Stretch Out With...

Bass & Drums, Blues & Standards

3060

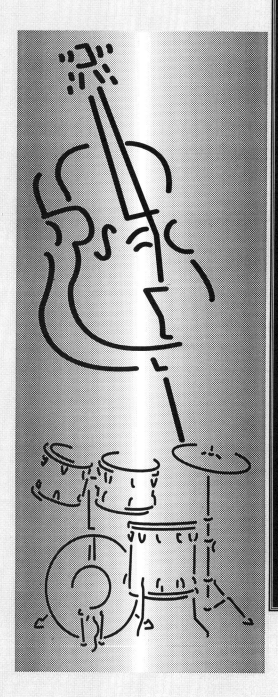

Charleston Blues
Lullaby Of The Leaves
Yancey Special
Blues In The Night
Latin Scene
Circle Of 4 Blues
Polka Dot Story
Cha-Cha
Foggy Baron
Now's The Time
Low Down Blues
Waltz Time Blues
Medium Blues in G
Body And Soul
How High The Moon
How About You
The Man I Love
April In Paris
It's Alright With Me
Slow Blues in F

Printed in Canada

MMO CD 3060

Music Minus One

Stretch Out With...
Bass & Drums, Blues & Standards

Charleston Blues

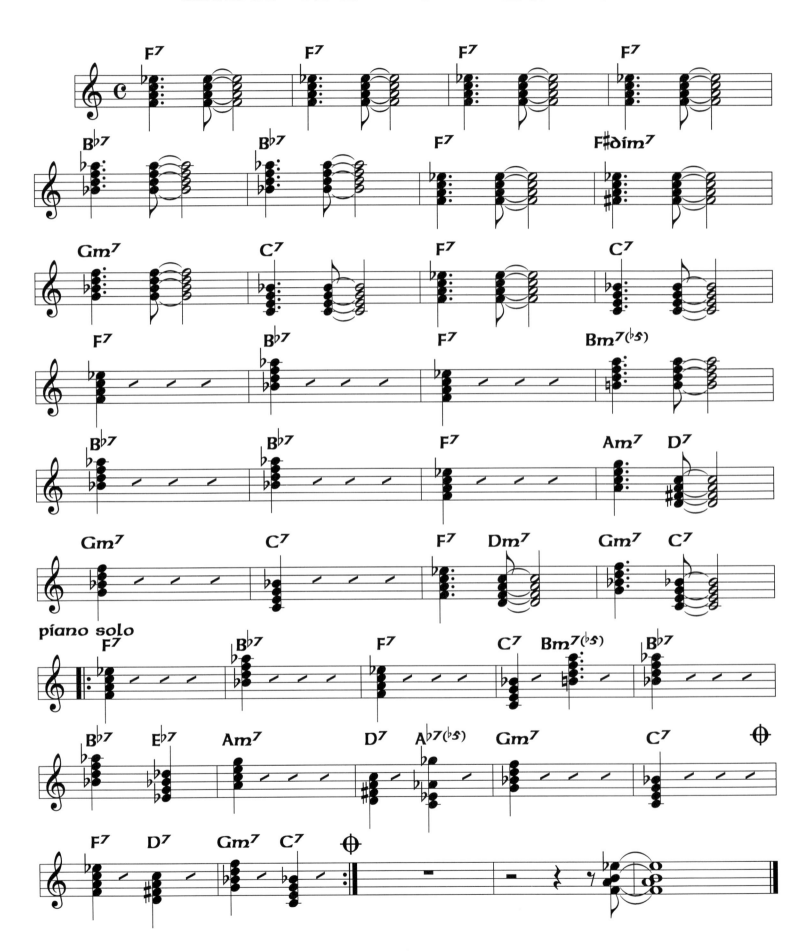

Lullaby Of The Leaves

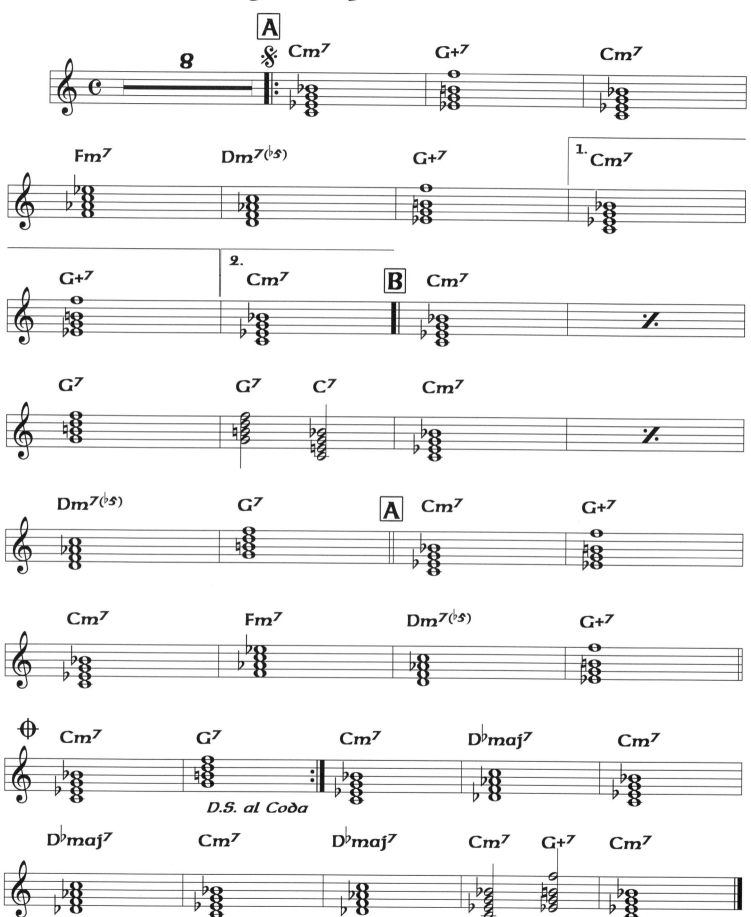

Yancey's Special

Blues In The Night

Latín Scene

"Circle Of 4" Blues

Polka Dot Story

Cha-Cha

Foggy Baron

Now's The Time

Low Down Blues

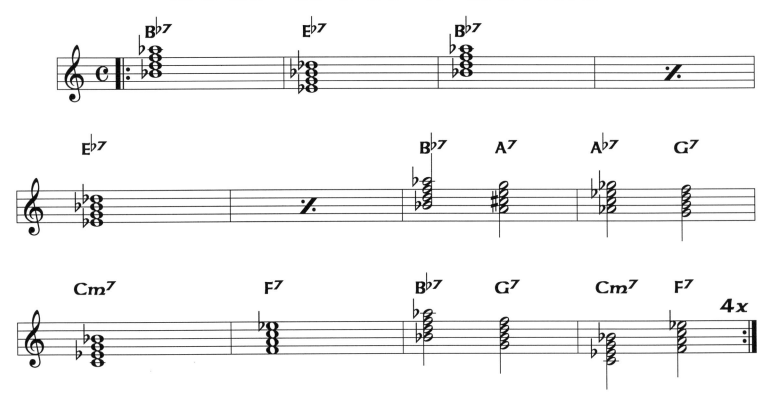

Waltz

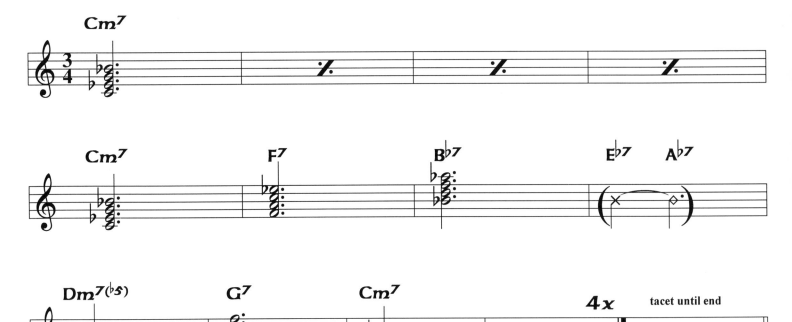

Medium Blues in G

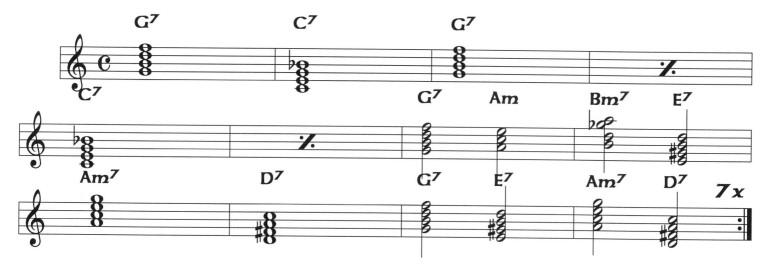

Body And Soul

How High The Moon

MO CD 3060

How About You

The Man I Love

MMO CD 3060

April In Paris

It's Alright With Me

MMO CD 3060

Slow Blues in F

Stretch Out With...

Bass & Drums, Blues & Standards

3060

Charleston Blues
Lullaby Of The Leaves
Yancey Special
Blues In The Night
Latin Scene
Circle Of 4 Blues
Polka Dot Story
Cha-Cha
Foggy Baron
Now's The Time
Low Down Blues
Waltz Time Blues
Medium Blues in G
Body And Soul
How High The Moon
How About You
The Man I Love
April In Paris
It's Alright With Me
Slow Blues in F

MUSIC MINUS ONE 50 Executive Boulevard ▪ Elmsford, New York 10523-1325